Combat Sports

GAIL TERP

Bolt is published by Black Rabbit Books
P.O. Box 227, Mankato, Minnesota, 56002.
www.blackrabbitbooks.com

Rhea Magaro, designer;
Alissa Thielges, editor

Library of Congress Cataloging-in-Publication Data
Names: Terp, Gail, 1951- author.
Title: MMA / by Gail Terp.
Other titles: Mixed martial arts
Description: Mankato, MN: Black Rabbit Books, 2025. | Series: Combat sports | Includes bibliographical references and index. | Audience: Ages 8-12 | Audience: Grades 4-6 | Summary: "Get ready for some intense grappling in this hi-lo nonfiction chapter book about mixed martial arts (MMA). Reluctant readers learn about important skills and gear needed to compete and will be inspired by champions in this combat sport"—Provided by publisher.
Identifiers: LCCN 2024011838 (print) | LCCN 2024011839 (ebook) | ISBN 9781644666852 (library binding) | ISBN 9781644667033 (ebook)
Subjects: LCSH: Mixed martial arts—Juvenile literature.
Classification: LCC GV1102.7.M59 T (print) | LCC GV1102.7.M59 (ebook) | DDC 796.815—dc23/eng/20240318
LC record available at https://lccn.loc.gov/2024011838

Image Credits

Alamy Stock Photo/Chris Willson, 24, Julian Murray, 26 (t), PxImages, 12–13, 27 (t), ZUMA Press, 26 (b), 27 (b); Dreamstime/Vitalij Sova, 11 (b); Getty Images/A-Digit, 22–23, Chris Unger, 4–5, 6–7, Cooper Neill, 20–21, Mikolette, 17 (t), peepo, 15 (t), skynesher, 11 (t), vm, 10 (b); Shutterstock/Andrey Burmakin, 10 (t), 15 (m), Andrii Zhmendak, 19, Andy Gin, 3, Artur Didyk, 28–29, El Nariz, 1, Geobor, cover, 32, Master1305, 15 (b), 18–19, Olga Popova, 19, oneinchpunch, 17 (b), Real Sports Photos, 22, Ruslan Shevchenko, 31, Slatan, 14, Stefan Holm, 8–9, Vitalii Demin, 22–23

Contents

CHAPTER 1

MMA in Action

In 2022, there was a big fight for mixed martial arts (MMA). Charles Oliveira held the lightweight **title**. Islam Makhachev wanted to take it from him.

Round one. The two fighters traded punches and kicks. Twice, they were on the mat, wrestling. Neither **dominated** the other.

UFC

Fighting for the Title

Round two. The fighters traded more strikes. Then Makhachev landed a hard punch. Oliviera fell to the mat. Quickly, Makhachev locked Oliveira in a **choke hold**. No longer able to fight, Oliviera gave up. He tapped the mat. Makhachev was the new champion!

An MMA champion earns a belt made of gold.

CHAPTER 2

What is MMA?

MMA is a mix of combat sports. The moves come from boxing and wrestling. They also come from kickboxing and Brazilian Jiu-Jitsu. Fighters can punch and kick. They can strike with their elbows and knees. Or they can grab their **opponents** and throw them.

MMA can be **brutal**. In fact, some places ban it. New rules have made MMA safer. Since 2016, it has been allowed in all US states. But fights are still banned in places in Canada.

Styles Used in MMA

Boxing

Brazilian Jiu-Jitsu

Kickboxing
Wrestling

Attack Moves

MMA has many attack moves. Fighters strike with hands and elbows. They kick with their feet and legs. And they **grapple** opponents to the ground. Fighters want to get opponents on the mat. That's called a takedown. Then they can get on top of the fighter. That's a strong position for winning the fight.

30
UFC

Defensive Moves

Attack moves are important. But a strong **defense** is too. Fighters use blocks to stop hits. High blocks protect the face. Low blocks protect the lower body. Blocking with a kick is called checking. In a parry, a fighter pushes a punch aside before it hits.

blocks: hands,
arms, elbows
checks: shins,
knees
parry:
hands, arms

CHAPTER 3

Winning a Match

MMA fighters train hard. They have many skills to learn. And they need to be good at all of them. They must build their strength. They must increase their **endurance**. To be successful, fighters train many hours a week.

Training for MMA has many benefits. It puts athletes in top physical shape.

MMA PRACTICE GEAR

SHIN GUARDS

protect lower legs

GLOVES

protect hands and fingers

HEADGEAR
protects head and face
MOUTHGUARD
protects mouth and teeth

Winning

There are four ways to win an MMA match. Fighters can trap opponents until they tap out. This is a submission win. Knockouts (KO) are when opponents get knocked down and can't get up. At times, a referee steps in. They decide if a fighter can't defend themselves. These are technical knockouts (TKO).

Some fights go all the rounds. They have no submission, KO, or TKO. Then the judges decide who wins.

MMA
WEIGHT
CLASSES
WOMEN
STRAWWEIGHT
MEN FLYWEIGHT
Up to 115
POUNDS
(52.2 kg)
115 to 125
POUNDS
(52.2 to 56.7 kg)
LOWEST WEIGHT CLASS

Fight Rules

Fighters are grouped in weight classes. This keeps fights fair. Fights have three or five rounds. Each round lasts five minutes.

An MMA fight has three judges. They score the fighters' moves with points. When judges must decide the winner, they use these points.

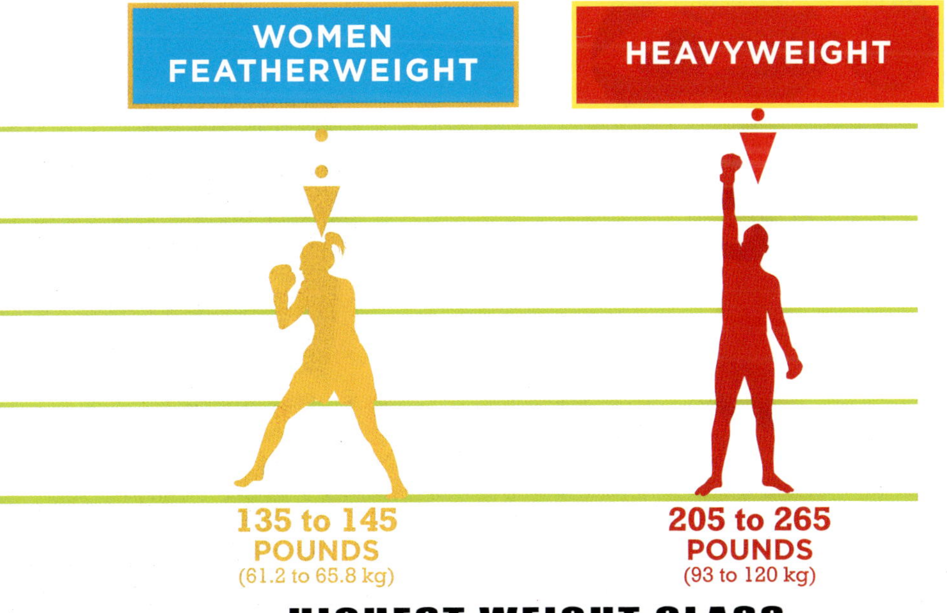

HIGHEST WEIGHT CLASS

UFC fighters fight in a cage with eight sides. It's called "The Octagon."

CHAPTER 4

MMA Competitions

The International Mixed Martial Arts Federation (IMMAF) is for **amateurs**. It holds world championships each year. Fighters can start at age 12. Many top fighters go on to fight as **professionals**.

There are many pro MMA groups. One is the Ultimate Fighting Championship (UFC). Fighters come from all over the world. People watch the fights on TV.

Demetrious Johnson

is an American. People call him "Mighty Mouse" because of his small size. He's been a UFC champion many times.

Stamp Fairtex

is from Thailand. She started martial arts training at age five. She's won an Atomweight World Championship.

Islam Makhachev

is from Russia. He's won the UFC Lightweight Championship. In 2023, he was voted MMA Fighter of the Year.

Cris "Cyborg" Santos

is from Brazil. She has won four championships. She helps other women train in martial arts.

By the Numbers

1 SECOND

FASTEST MMA KNOCKOUT

19 YEARS OLD

age of youngest MMA world champion, Angela Lee

4
OUNCES
(113 G)
AVERAGE WEIGHT OF AN MMA GLOVE
1990s
THE BEGINNING OF MODERN MMA
1
MINUTE
LENGTH OF REST TIME BETWEEN ROUNDS

GLOSSARY

amateur (AM-uh-chur)—not professional

brutal (BROOT-l)—extremely hard or mean

choke hold (CHOHK HOHLD)—holding your arm around someone's neck with enough pressure to make breathing difficult

defense (DEE-fens)—a way of resisting attack

dominate (DOM-uh-neyt)—to hold a commanding position over someone

endurance (en-DOOR-uhns)—the ability to put up with strain, suffering, or hardship

grapple (GRAP-uhl)—to hold and fight with another person

opponent (uh-POH-nunt)—a person, team, or group that is competing against another

professional (pro-FESH-uh-nuhl)—paid to compete in a sport or activity

round (ROUND)—one of a series of events

title (TAHYT-l)—the championship

BOOKS

Bolt Simons, Lisa M. *Curious about Martial Arts.* Mankato, MN: Amicus Learning, 2024.

Krohn, Frazer Andrew. *MMA: Ferocious Fighting Styles.* Minneapolis: Abdo Publishing, 2023.

WEBSITES

Mixed Martial Arts
kids.britannica.com/students/article/mixed-martial-arts-MMA/626791

Mixed Martial Arts Facts for Kids
kids.kiddle.co/Mixed_martial_arts

What Are Martial Arts?
www.wonderopolis.org/wonder/What-Are-Martial-Arts

INDEX